Published by:
Olive Tree Meditations,
Chesham,
Buckinghamshire.
www.olive-tree-meditations.co.uk

Scripture quotations are taken from:
The HOLY BIBLE, NEW INTERNATIONAL VERSION.
Copyright © 1973, 1978, 1984 by International Bible Society.
Used by permission.

ISBN 978-1-7399845-0-2

The book is set in Cochin, with Silentium Pro used for the chapter headings.

Printed by Orbitpress Ltd.,
Chesham, Buckinghamshire, U.K.

A PLACE OF GRACE

A Collection of Illuminated Meditations

Helen White

'Therefore, since we have been justified through faith,
we have peace with God through our Lord Jesus Christ,
through whom we have gained access by faith
into this grace in which we now stand . . .'

Romans 5 v 1 - 2

CONTENTS

INTRODUCTION

Illumination

'Illumination' - what a wonderful word! It speaks of bringing light to dark places. Almighty God is the supreme 'Illuminator':
'In the beginning God created the heavens and the earth. Now the earth was formless and empty, darkness was over the surface of the deep, and the Spirit of God was hovering over the waters.
And God said, "Let there be light," and there was light.' (Genesis 1 v 1-3)

. . . and with light comes life:
'In the beginning was the Word, and the Word was with God, and the Word was God . . . In him was life, and that life was the light of men.'
(John 1 v 1 & 4)

Our Lord Jesus Christ said: 'I am the light of the world. Whoever follows me will never walk in darkness, but will have the light of life.' (John 8 v 12)

'Illumination' is derived from the Latin *'illuminare'*, 'to give light' or 'to light up', and can be used to mean the bringing of actual light to a place of darkness, or to give spiritual or intellectual understanding.

In this book I have both these meanings of the word *'illumination'* in mind:

- When we read God's Word we pray and ask for the Holy Spirit to help us, 'illuminating' our reading of the Bible to bring the light of spiritual understanding, and how it applies to our lives. The Psalmist understood the truth of this, writing of his own experience: 'Your word is a lamp to my feet and a light for my path . . . The unfolding of your words gives light; it gives understanding to the simple.' (Psalm 119 v 105 and 130)

- In the context of the artwork, the use of gold (or other metal) is called 'Illumination'. Think of one of the beautiful medieval manuscripts of the Scriptures, richly embellished with gold to honour God. From some angles  the gold appears to be mid-brown in colour. Now imagine the pages being turned: the gold catches the candlelight and lights up: it 'illuminates' the page. The contrast can be seen in these details from one of my 'illuminated rose windows' (right and left).

Reflection and Meditation

In order for the Holy Spirit to shed his light and illuminate our understanding, we need to take time to reflect, or meditate, on God's Word in humility and openness. We need to sit under His word rather than impose our ideas on it, or distort it to say what we would like to hear.

Throughout the Bible reference is made to meditating on God's words, character and actions. Joshua was told: 'Do not let this Book of the Law depart from your mouth; meditate on it day and night . . . ' (Joshua 1 v 8).

The Psalmists often speak about meditation:
'Within your temple, O God, we meditate on your unfailing love.'
(Psalm 48 v 9)

'Let me understand the teaching of your precepts; then I will meditate on your wonders.' (Psalm 119 v 27)

'My eyes stay open through the watches of the night, that I may meditate on your promises.' (Psalm 119 v 148)

'I remember the days of long ago; I meditate on all your works and consider what your hands have done.' (Psalm 143 v 5)

When Mary heard what the shepherds had been told by the angels about the birth of a Saviour, and how they had been directed to the little family in the stable, while 'all who heard it were amazed . . . Mary treasured up all these things and pondered them in her heart.' (Luke 2 v 18 - 19)

Paul encouraged Timothy to: 'Reflect on what I am saying, for the Lord will give you insight into all this.' (2 Timothy 2 v 7)

What is meditation?
Meditation is about listening; listening for the 'still, small voice' of God, rather than studying the text. Studying the text is valuable and necessary, but in meditation we approach the words in a different way. The word 'meditate' can be translated or paired with 'consider', 'ponder' or 'think on'.

Meditation is like savouring the taste of a delicious meal, when we allow the flavours to linger on our palette, seeking to detect the various herbs or spices that have been used.
It is about having our attention caught by something that we had not noticed before, or focussing on a detail, dwelling on it, and examining it closely. We

may think about why we were drawn to that word or phrase in particular, and what God wants to teach us through it. We may be led to make a connection with another verse or passage, which adds to our understanding. Notice (from a number of references, eg: Psalm 1 v 2), that we are to meditate 'day and night'. Thinking about God's words and works is to provide the background rhythm for our life. It is as if they are a musical theme that we have on our mind all day, and we find ourselves humming it whatever we are doing. Sometimes a new realisation can come to us 'out of the blue', while we are occupied with something else - gardening or washing up, even! Memorising verses is very helpful in many ways, but it also means that we can meditate on God's word even when we do not have a Bible open in front of us, when we are out for a walk, for instance. As we read in Proverbs:

'Pay attention and listen to the sayings of the wise; apply your heart to what I teach, for it is pleasing when you keep them in your heart and have all of them ready on your lips.' (Proverbs 22 v 17 - 18)

Meditation is not just for when life is good and ticking along nicely; no, it is also for the difficult times. The Psalmists meditated on God and His word in the midst of trouble. When under pressure or in difficulty, the writer of Psalm 119 does not get overwhelmed by the situation; instead, he considers God's word: 'The wicked are waiting to destroy me, but I will ponder your statutes.' (Psalm 119 v 95).

And he is not going to be distracted by trying to defend or justify himself: 'May the arrogant be put to shame for wronging me without cause; but I will meditate on your precepts' (Psalm 119 v 78)

Indeed, the way through a difficult time, and to not be overwhelmed by a situation, is to lift our eyes to the One who is on the throne: 'On the glorious splendour of your majesty and on your wonderful works I will meditate.' (Psalm 145 v 5, alternative text) Many psalms that begin with a plea for help and deliverance finish with words of praise to God and trust in His faithfulness.

In the midst of his suffering, Job was challenged and encouraged to ' . . . stop and consider God's wonders.' (Job 37 v 14)

In order to reflect on God's Word we need quality time in a quiet place. This can be something that some people never find because they are too focussed on 'externals' - material possessions, social media etc.. It is not easy; however, it is worth pursuing, for we can know great blessing through these times.

The writing that accompanies each Illumination is intended as a starting point for your own contemplation of the painting and accompanying verses. The Place of Grace is a place where we encounter God: may the thoughts of your hearts be illuminated by the Holy Spirit.

Geometry and Symbolism

Many of these pieces of artwork use geometry as their structural basis, which brings harmony and beauty to the design. Geometry underpins Creation, from the tiniest flower (and smaller) to the movement of the planets. God established order in Creation, and without Him life becomes chaos.

Medieval craftsmen regarded geometry as a reflection of the beauty of Divine order in Creation, and the aim of ecclesiastical art and architecture from that time was to reveal this beauty and point towards God. True 'Sacred Art' is so much more than just a 'religious illustration'; it should be like a window onto heaven, showing us, or reminding us of, something that is true about God.

The symbolism used in the work of medieval craftsmen often goes unnoticed today because the meaning is ignored or forgotten. A 'symbol' is something which represents something else - an idea, thought, doctrine or truth. It reflects something higher, and is used to assist our understanding of what is represented.

Traditional Sacred Art conveys spiritual truths by depicting one thing, while inviting the viewer to see something else, something deeper: the spiritual significance and truth. Through contemplation, looking deeper with the eyes of the heart, the symbol helps us to understand that which it represents. A symbol should also help us to remember the truth it represents, for example, the lamb in the Jewish Passover festival, and the bread and wine of Holy Communion.

Another simple example is a trefoil shape being a reminder of the Trinity. Every time we see a three petalled flower in the garden, or a three-fold carving, we can remember the triune God: Father, Son and Holy Spirit: Three in One.

Traditionally, a circle represents heaven: it is formed by a continuous line, without beginning or end. Our own experience of the sky is to see the line of the horizon forming a circle around us. The number four, and therefore, a square, is associated with the earth: there are four compass directions, four elements and four seasons that give rhythm to the year. Revelation 7 v 1 speaks of ' . . . the four corners of the earth.'

In the writing accompanying each piece I explain the symbolism used. During the medieval period the Church became somewhat overloaded with symbols, which sometimes led to a distortion or misunderstanding of the Truth, or became mixed up with superstition. At the Reformation, the use of imagery was stripped back, but a rich seam of material for contemplation was lost. I hope that the symbolism I have used is helpful and 'illuminating', rather than a distraction, and that this, in turn, will inspire further insights to open hearts.

Grace

'GRACE' is such a beautiful word, and it is central to the Christian faith. It conveys the truth that we simply don't deserve what God is so willing to freely give: life, true life, eternal life: we are forgiven and made whole.

Grace is the golden thread that runs through the whole Bible from Genesis to Revelation - God's love shown to undeserving people: the promise in Genesis 3 of One who would crush Satan's head; the favour shown to Noah and his family; the covenants with Abraham, Isaac and Jacob; the rescue of Israel from slavery in Egypt (with the Passover foreshadowing the promised salvation through Christ); the way God always preserved a 'remnant' of faithful people through all the ups and downs of the people of Israel as described in the Old Testament . . . until the promises of a Saviour found their fulfilment in the life, death and resurrection of our Lord Jesus Christ, the supreme expression of God's grace.

The extravagance and generosity of this love is astounding. No wonder John exclaimed, "How great is the love the Father has lavished on us, that we should be called children of God!" (1 John 3 v 1)
And Paul wrote: 'But because of his great love for us, God, who is rich in mercy, made us alive with Christ even when we were dead in transgressions - it is by grace you have been saved.' (Ephesians 2 v 4 - 5)

Grace and Mercy are often used interchangeably, but there is an important distinction which needs to be made. God shows His GRACE when He gives us what we don't deserve. God shows His MERCY when He doesn't give us what we do deserve.

"For God so loved the world that he gave his one and only Son, that whoever believes in him shall not perish but have eternal life. For God did not send his Son into the world to condemn the world, but to save the world through him." (John 3 v 16 - 17)

We deserve to be condemned by God because of our sin, but in His mercy He gives us the opportunity to repent and be forgiven by faith in Jesus' death and resurrection. Even this faith is not from ourselves, 'it is the gift of God'. (Ephesians 2 v 8) We cannot earn mercy or grace by doing good things; they are undeserved gifts from God, if we will but accept them . . .

'But now a righteousness from God, apart from law, has been made known, to which the Law and the Prophets testify. This righteousness from God comes through faith in Jesus Christ to all who believe. There is no difference, for all have sinned and fall short of the glory of God, and are justified freely by his grace through the redemption that came by Christ Jesus.' (Romans 3 v 21 - 24)

A PLACE OF
GRACE

Pause . . . and enter

A Place of Grace

Gold leaf, shell gold and watercolour on paper

A PLACE OF GRACE

The starting point for this collection of Illuminated Meditations is a piece which grew out of a project that was set as part of my Master's Degree in Traditional Art: we were to design a Sanctuary, whatever we perceived a 'Sanctuary' to be. I chose to design a private place set aside for prayer, contemplation and quietness. It was a walled garden; more specifically, a cloister garden.

Since drawing the original design, I feel it has come to represent so much more than simply a *place* of prayer. It has different facets, and can be seen from different angles: as well as a place to pray, it is also a picture of the Christian life, and indeed, of prayer itself.

The Geometry of the Cloister Garden

All the main structural elements are related geometrically; this gives them a proportional harmony (see below, left). The entrance opens into a covered walkway, an octagonal cloister. However, the gap in the balustrade for entry into the central garden area is not directly opposite the door; it is round on the far side, to encourage a 'slowing down' before entering the garden. (See below, right.)

A Picture of the Christian Life

In medieval times, the Hortus Conclusus, or 'enclosed garden', was a spiritual picture of the soul consecrated to God: set apart for God and, therefore, distinct from the world around.

The term 'Cloister' is from the Latin 'claustrum', meaning 'enclosure'. An enclosed garden is a safe and protected place. Think of David's words: 'You hem me in - behind and before; you have laid your hand upon me . . . Where can I go from your Spirit? Where can I flee from your presence?' (Psalm 139 v 5 & 7)

I do not see this as a claustrophobic or unwelcome restriction, but as an assurance of safety and security. As David also wrote: 'The boundary lines have fallen for me in pleasant places; surely I have a delightful inheritance.' (Psalm 16 v 6)

In Romans 5 v 1 - 2 we read: 'Therefore, since we have been justified through faith, we have peace with God through our Lord Jesus Christ, through whom we have gained access by faith into this grace in which we now stand . . .'

Through faith we have gained access into grace, God's grace: 'this grace in which we now stand.' This phrase was the inspirational starting point for this collection of paintings and writing: when we put our trust in Jesus Christ as our Lord and Saviour, we enter into a 'Place of Grace', and in that place we live and move and have our being. This Grace from heaven follows us throughout our lives, as a spotlight follows an actor around the stage. This is true not just when we pray or go to Church, but **all the time.**

'One thing I ask of the LORD, this is what I seek:
that I may dwell in the house of the LORD all the days of my life,
to gaze upon the beauty of the LORD and to seek him in his temple.'
(Psalm 27 v 4)

Thanks be to God, that this can be true for us, because He has made it possible for us to enter and live our lives in this Place of Grace. Note that the Psalmist asks to 'dwell' in the house of the Lord, not just visit occasionally: we live in God's presence all the time.

What is more, Jesus, the Good Shepherd, reassures us that once we have put our trust in Him, outward influences cannot remove us from His care, or that of our Heavenly Father: 'My sheep listen to my voice; I know them, and they follow me. I give them eternal life, and they shall never perish; no-one can snatch them out of my hand. My Father, who has given them to me, is greater than all; no-one can snatch them out of my Father's hand'.
(John 10 v 27 - 29)
How wonderful to know that we cannot accidentally slip out of this Place of Grace: we are totally safe in our Heavenly Father's hands.
Nowhere is beyond the reach of God's Spirit and presence; we cannot be separated from His love: Paul encourages us with his conviction that there is nothing in all creation that ' . . . will be able to separate us from the love of God that is in Christ Jesus our Lord.' (See Romans 8 v 38 - 39)

So the cloister garden is a picture of the blessed state of the Christian soul, safe in the love of God, through Jesus Christ our Lord. No matter what difficulties we might have to face in this present world, we remain in this Place of Grace, even though there may be times when our life might feel more like a 'war zone'.

In one sense, we live in this Place of Grace all the time: it is where we dwell as Christian people. In another sense, it is our place of prayer and communion with God, and we can quietly slip in, without anyone knowing, even in the midst of busyness. In the painting, we could imagine that the day-to-day living of our lives takes place in the covered walkway, but when we take time with God, we step into the garden in the centre of the cloister.

'I delight greatly in the Lord; my soul rejoices in my God. For he has clothed me with garments of salvation and arrayed me in a robe of righteousness . . '
(Isaiah 61 v 10a)

What a lovely picture of the blessing of a relationship with God: knowing that we are reconciled to Him and in a right standing with Him - not through our own efforts to be good or by keeping rules and rituals, but through faith in our Lord Jesus Christ, who lived and died and rose again to bring us into this Place of Grace. Truly, faith is a precious gift!

What are we to do in this Place of Grace? - Paul continues - 'And we rejoice in the hope of the glory of God. Not only so, but we also rejoice in our sufferings, because we know that suffering produces perseverance; perseverance, character; and character, hope. And hope does not disappoint us, because God has poured out his love into our hearts by the Holy Spirit, whom he has given us.' (Romans 5 v 2b - 5)

We are to rejoice because of God's grace to us, and the hope that this gives us. With regard to his words about suffering, I don't think Paul means that we should rejoice that we are suffering, but that even in the midst of suffering we can rejoice because we know that we are not alone. He also reminds us that there are types of suffering that can actually help us to mature as people, and grow in our faith.

'Blessed are those who dwell in your house; they are ever praising you.' (Psalm 84 v 4)

A Picture of a Place of Prayer

Of course, we can pray wherever we are, but many people have a favourite place that they use for prayer, and that can be very helpful: it may be a particular chair or room; it may be in a church or at home, in the garden or on a walk. It is the place we go to when we wish to take special time with God, and we associate it with prayer: it becomes a Place of Grace, a place where we encounter God.

For some people, finding a quiet place, or the time, may be difficult. Knowing how important it is to take time with the Lord in prayer, Susannah Wesley made the time and the place: when her (many) children saw her sitting with her apron pulled up over her head, they knew they should not disturb her, for she was praying. For some, a train journey may be the time when they close their eyes and pray. Even a short time is better than no time:

'Better is one day in your courts than a thousand elsewhere; I would rather be a doorkeeper in the house of my God than dwell in the tents of the wicked.' (Psalm 84 v 10)

We need to read and reflect and pray, asking God to illuminate our understanding and help us to readjust our focus to gain a godly perspective on things. Then we can face difficulties and challenges with the strength that God alone can give. Let us heed the words of the Psalmist:

'I have set the LORD always before me. Because he is at my right hand, I shall not be shaken.' (Psalm 16 v 8)

In a monastery, the cloisters are not only a place of prayer, but they are also part of the everyday living environment. Similarly, we are not to be cut off from the world and everyday life. However, if we are to be 'in the world, but not of the world', we need to have a place of peace, a place of quiet, away from all the busyness around us, for prayer and reflection.

In the Gospels we read of Jesus himself going out to a solitary place to pray, and He also knew when His disciples needed to take time to recharge: 'Then, because so many people were coming and going that they did not even have a chance to eat, [Jesus said to the disciples], "Come with me by yourselves to a quiet place and get some rest." So they went away by themselves in a boat to a solitary place.' (Mark 6 v 31 - 32)
Similarly, we need to take time by ourselves, with Jesus; to do so is to enter into a Place of Grace.

Of course we can pray wherever we are, but if we are not in particularly beautiful surroundings, we may wish to imagine that we are in a garden.

A Picture of Prayer

Finally, this piece is also meant as a picture of Prayer itself. Wherever we are, we can enter this Place of Grace called Prayer. Sometimes we find ourselves in a difficult situation, and we offer an 'arrow prayer' asking for help or wisdom: 'God is our refuge and strength, an ever-present help in trouble . . "Be still, and know that I am God . . ." ' (Psalm 46 v 1 & 10), and we can do this even when all around us is noise and activity and busyness: in our heart we can enter that Place of Grace called Prayer, and know that God is God.

While we are to 'pray continually' (1 Thessalonians 5 v 17), it is also valuable to set aside quality time for prayer, when we can be quiet, meditate on God's Word, and listen for His 'still small voice'. This is what I have pictured as a garden: it is being with God. It is a wonderful privilege to be able to come to Almighty God in prayer: 'Let us then approach the throne of grace with confidence, so that we may receive mercy and find grace to help us in our time of need.' (Hebrews 4 v 16)

To enter into Prayer is to enter into a Place of Grace, before the Throne of Grace.

Prayer will, of course, take different forms: praise, worship, confession, thanksgiving, petition and supplication, as well as contemplation and meditation on the Word of God, and, of course, these include listening.

"Do not be anxious about anything, but in everything, by prayer and petition, with thanksgiving, present your requests to God. And the peace of God, which transcends all understanding, will guard you hearts and minds in Christ Jesus." (Philippians 4 v 6 - 7)

19

Description of the Cloister and Garden

A beautiful garden is a wonderful place to be, with sights and sounds, fragrances and peace. The beautiful flowers inspire us to praise our Creator; we may catch the scent of these blooms, often just fleetingly, wafting through the air; butterflies flutter through while we hear the birds singing and water gently gurgling in the fountain. At certain times we may be able to enjoy freshly picked fruit.

Most monastic cloisters are square; my design is octagonal. One reason for this is that the number eight is seen as a transitional number: In a square building with a circular dome, the easiest form of  transition from square to circle (ie: between the top of the walls and the base of the dome), is via an octagon. Traditionally, a square is associated with the earth, and a circle with heaven (see page 10). An octagon 'mediates', and provides the transition between the square and the circle; it is where they touch. Our Lord Jesus Christ mediates between God and Humanity, between heaven and earth. An octagon would, therefore, seem to be an appropriate shape for a place of prayer: a place on earth where we focus on 'things above, where Christ is seated at the right hand of God.' (Colossians 3 v 1)

The door into the Sanctuary is narrow. It is not a wide, double door that is opened with pomp and ceremony, as on the day of a great procession. Although it is the door to life, it is a narrow door, and reminds us of Jesus' words: 'Enter through the narrow gate. For wide is the gate and broad is the road that leads to destruction, and many enter through it. But small is the gate and narrow the road that leads to life, and only a few find it.' (Matthew 7 v 13 - 14)

Around the door into the cloister a Passion Flower grows. It is a reminder that it is only through the Passion of our Lord Jesus Christ on the cross that we are able to approach Almighty God. (See 'Illuminated Rose Window - Passiflora', page 51 for further significance of the Passion Flower).

Upon entering the door into the cloister walkway itself, we find that the way into the central garden is actually on the far side of the cloister. We cannot rush straight into the garden in the centre: we need to walk around the covered path, slowing down and stilling our thoughts. How easy it is to rush into prayer, unprepared, and immediately launch into our requests for help, without taking time to slow down and remember into Whose presence we have come.

The cloister encloses an open courtyard garden, and at the centre of this is a planting area in the shape of a cross. The Cross is at the centre of this Place of Grace, just as the Cross of Christ is at the centre of the Christian faith, at the centre of our prayers, and indeed, of all that we do. It is only through the cross that we can enter at all.

We come to the cross for forgiveness, humbly acknowledging our sin and our need for a Saviour: ' . . . for all have sinned and fall short of the glory of God, and are justified freely by his grace through the redemption that came by Christ Jesus. God presented him as a sacrifice of atonement, through faith in his blood . . .' (Romans 3 v 23 - 25)

In the centre of the cross-shaped planting area is a gentle, bubbling fountain. The fountain reminds us that we come to the cross for cleansing from our sin, and also for refreshment: the living water that is found in Christ:

Jesus said, '"If anyone is thirsty, let him come to me and drink. Whoever believes in me, as the Scripture has said, streams of living water will flow from within him." By this he meant the Spirit, whom those who believed in him were later to receive.' (John 7 v 37 - 39)

'"Surely God is my salvation; I will trust and not be afraid. The LORD, the LORD, is my strength and my song; he has become my salvation." With joy you will draw water from the wells of salvation.' (Isaiah 12 v 2 - 3)

Symbolism of the plants used

Certain plants have symbolic significance and can teach or remind us of spiritual truths.

Almond Tree - The Almond represents resurrection because it is the first tree in the Near East to flower, or 'wake up'. The Hebrew for 'almond tree' sounds like the Hebrew for 'watching' or 'to be wakeful'. In Jeremiah we read: 'The word of the LORD came to me: "What do you see, Jeremiah?" "I see the branch of an almond tree," I replied. The LORD said to me, "You have seen correctly, for I am watching to see that my word is fulfilled."' (Jeremiah 1 v 11 - 12) God is watchful and faithful, ensuring that His word is fulfilled.

Almond flowers also featured on the Lampstand in the Tabernacle: its flower-like cups were shaped like almond blossom. The Lampstand stood in the Holy Place, where the lights were kept burning all through the night, a reminder of the constant, wakeful faithfulness of the Lord watching over His people.

We must be watchful, as well: as Jesus warned Peter: 'Watch and pray so that you will not fall into temptation. The spirit is willing, but the body is weak.' (Matthew 26 v 41); and Paul challenged Timothy: 'Watch your life and doctrine closely. Persevere in them . . . ' (1 Timothy 4 v 16)

Heartsease/Viola - In medieval herbals (books describing the properties and usage of herbs), the wild pansy (viola tricolor) was dedicated to the Trinity and known as 'Herba Trinitas', because of the three colours of its flowers. Its common name, 'Heartsease', springs from the belief that diseases of the heart would improve with an infusion of the plant - including the mending of a broken heart. This aside, its beautiful, dainty flowers certainly bring joy to the heart!

Lavender - This is not mentioned in the Bible, but traditionally its flowers have come to represent qualities such as purity, serenity, silence, devotion, calmness and grace, so it seems an appropriate plant for this garden. Of course, its wonderful fragrance makes it a lovely addition to the space.

Olive Tree - The Hebrew word for olive/olive tree can also refer to the oil that it yields, which was used in lamps to provide light - it is 'illuminating oil!' Another Hebrew word for olive can also mean to 'shine' or 'anoint'. Therefore, this tree can remind us that Jesus is the source of spiritual illumination; He said: 'I am the light of the world. Whoever follows me will never walk in darkness, but will have the light of life.' (John 8 v 12)

Jesus also said that His followers would reflect His light to the world: 'You are the light of the world . . . people [do not] light a lamp and put it under a bowl. Instead they put it on its stand, and it gives light to everyone in the house. In the same way, let your light shine before men, that they may see your good deeds and praise your Father in heaven.' (Matthew 5 v 14 - 16)

Orange Tree - Planted for the wonderful fragrance from its blossom, and delicious fruit.

Pinks - Included for the lovely clove-like scent of the flowers.

Pomegranate Tree - Pomegranates formed part of the Temple ornament (see 1 Kings 7 v 18), possibly as a symbol of fruitfulness, because of its many seeds, and they also adorned the hem of the robe of the high priest, made of blue, purple and scarlet yarn (see Exodus 28 v 33). In the Old Testament we find a foreshadowing of the New Covenant that is fulfilled in Christ, and He is now in heaven as our great high priest (see Hebrews 4 v 14-16; 7 v 25, 27; 8 v 2, 6). So what can the colours of the pomegranates on the robe be a reminder of?

Blue is a symbol of heaven, and of Jesus' divinity - He came from heaven in the incarnation, and ascended to heaven after the resurrection.

Scarlet is the colour of sacrifice: Christ's sacrifice on the cross to win our salvation.

Purple is the colour of royalty, and Jesus reigns as King over all. The fruit has a crown-like calyx on top, which can lead us to reflect on Christ's Kingship over his Church.

A Pomegranate can also symbolise the Church: one fruit containing many seeds, which represent the believers who make up the universal Church (see 1 Corinthians 12 v 12 - 31).

Rose - According to Ambrose (4th century bishop of Milan), the rose had no thorns in the Garden of Eden, until after the Fall. While there is, of course, nothing to imply this in the Bible, we can still enjoy the beauty of the flowers, and their perfume. We can also look at the thorns and reflect on how devastating the effect of sin is, and also see them as a reminder of Jesus' crown of thorns, and ponder His victory over sin on the cross.

Shamrock - Symbolises the Trinity, being one leaf, made up of three separate leaflets.

Strawberry - The three-fold leaf can represent the Trinity, while the five sepals can be a reminder of the five wounds of the crucified Christ. The red fruit can call to mind the blood of Jesus. It is a small plant that grows close to the ground, and so can be symbolic of humility.

Violet - This dainty little flower symbolises humility because it grows close to the ground, often under larger plants and hedges. Thus it can be a reminder of the humility of Jesus: 'Who, being in very nature God, did not consider equality with God something to be grasped, but made himself nothing, taking the very nature of a servant, being made in human likeness. And . . . He humbled himself and became obedient to death - even death on a cross!' (Philippians 2 v 6 - 8)

Willow Tree - This can symbolise the Gospel message because it can be severely trimmed but keeps growing back. Similarly, the spread of God's Word (and His Church), cannot be stopped: in spite of persecution, the faith of Christians and the Church continue to grow.

As this piece developed, and when the flowers were painted in, they seemed to shine out like jewels! This is a reminder that through prayer and time taken with God, we can discover the 'jewels' of what it means to be one of His people. We can ponder the riches of salvation, and the treasures that are His promises to us in His word.

So let us *take* time and *make* time to enter this Place of Grace, and delight to be with our Lord.
'Trust in the Lord and do good; dwell in the land and enjoy safe pasture.
Delight yourself in the Lord and he will give you the desires of your heart.'
(Psalm 37 v 3 - 4)

Carpet Page

Gold leaf and watercolour with sapphires and pearls

CARPET PAGE

A Carpet Page is a page in a manuscript which is purely decoration; it has no words, and is so called because it is reminiscent of carpet designs. In the Lindisfarne Gospels, a wonderful manuscript made in Northumbria in the early eighth century, each of the four Gospels is preceded by a carpet page. Prayer mats were known to have been used in Northumbria at this time, so it could be that these carpet pages are intended as a reminder to the reader to prepare themselves, and of the need to approach the pages that follow them (ie: the Gospels) with prayerful humility, for they are none other than the very words of God.

'Guard your steps when you go to the house of God. Go near to listen rather than to offer the sacrifice of fools, who do not know that they do wrong.

Do not be quick with your mouth, do not be hasty in your heart to utter anything before God.

God is in heaven and you are on earth, so let your words be few.'
(Ecclesiastes 5 v 1 - 2)

Yet how can we, as sinful human beings, approach God, who burns with holiness? In the Lindisfarne Gospels the four Carpet Pages are each based on a different style of cross, thus reminding us that we can only approach the Throne of Grace through the Cross of Christ. It is worth reflecting on this before launching into prayer. It should give us the proper perspective as we come to the Place of Grace that is Prayer.

'For it is by grace you have been saved, through faith - and this not from yourselves, it is the gift of God - not by works, so that no-one can boast.'
(Ephesians 2 v 8 - 9)

This design for a Carpet Page is also based on a cross, and the patterns are inspired by those found in medieval Armenian manuscript illumination. The pearls speak of the perfection of Christ's sacrifice on the cross.

The carpet pages found in early manuscripts also recall metalwork of the time, and so symbolise the Crux Gemmata, the jewelled cross. In early Christian art this speaks of the second coming of Christ.

'Let us then approach the throne of grace with confidence, so that we may receive mercy and find grace to help us in our time of need.' (Hebrews 4 v 16)

A Prayer:

'"O worship the Lord in the beauty of holiness . . .' . . . but how can I, Lord, sinful being that I am? I should turn and leave, lest I intrude unworthily . . . and yet I cannot leave; I must stay, for only with You is there forgiveness and life: I exclaim with Peter: 'Lord, to whom shall we go? You have the words of eternal life.' (John 6 v 68)

Thank you, Lord, that You make good what I lack: by faith in the blood of Christ, I am clothed with the righteousness of Christ, and therefore I may stay and worship. Amen."

The Light Shines in the Darkness . . .

Platinum leaf, palladium leaf, shell palladium and watercolour on paper

with sapphires and pearl

THE LIGHT SHINES IN THE DARKNESS . . .

'In the beginning was the Word, and the Word was with God, and the Word was God. He was with God in the beginning.
Through him all things were made; without him nothing was made that has been made. In him was life, and that life was the light of men. The light shines in the darkness, but the darkness has not understood it . . .

The true light that gives light to every man was coming into the world.
He was in the world, and though the world was made through him, the world did not recognise him . . . Yet to all who received him, to those who believed in his name, he gave the right to become children of God . . .

The Word became flesh and made his dwelling among us. We have seen his glory, the glory of the One and Only, who came from the Father, full of grace and truth.' (John 1 v 1 - 5, 9 - 10, 12, 14)

The phrase, *'In the beginning . . . '* takes us back to the first page of the Bible. Every part of creation was spoken into being by God: 'And God said, "Let there be . . ."' (Genesis 1) and 'By the word of the LORD were the heavens made . . .' (Psalm 33 v 6). 'The Word of God' is God in action. The prophets were given understanding and illumination when 'the Word of the LORD came to' them. (For example: Isaiah 38 v 4 and Jeremiah 1 v 4)

The Greek for 'the Word of God' is *'logos'*, and was used by Jews as an alternative way of referring to God, so that the Name of the Lord would not be uttered. For the Greeks, logos was the ordering principle in the universe.

In these verses, John asserts that Jesus is the Word. He is God, fully divine, *and yet he became flesh,* He became fully human, (though not ceasing to be fully divine), and *'made his dwelling among us'.* God had made His dwelling among His people Israel, in the Tabernacle in the desert and in the Temple in Jerusalem, but the people could not *'see'* Him, for they would have perished in His holiness . . . but Jesus dwelt in human form. He was 'Emmanuel, God with us', in order to achieve salvation, that we might become God's children.

Jesus gives life, true life: it is His gift to those who 'receive Him'.
Jesus said, 'I have come that they may have life, and have it to the full . . . I give them eternal life, and they shall never perish . . .' (John 10 v 10, 28)

Jesus is also light, and gives light, spiritual illumination, to those who come to Him for life. He said, 'I am the light of the world. Whoever follows me will never walk in darkness, but will have the light of life.' (John 8 v 12)

In verse 5, there are two alternative words for the response of the darkness to the light that is shining; they each supply insights to be considered. The first is that 'the darkness has not understood' the light. It is a sad fact that many people ignore the light: they ignore Jesus, and make no effort to look into His claims, or consider questions of life, death or eternity.

The second, (the alternative translation in the NIV footnote), is that 'the darkness has not overcome' the light. This is the wonderful affirmation that Jesus defeated sin and death through His death and resurrection. As Jesus said when He spoke of his forthcoming death, ' . . . now the prince of this world will be driven out.' (John 12 v 31). Although Jesus' death appeared to be Satan's victory, Jesus' resurrection proved otherwise: 'Death has been swallowed up in victory.' (1 Corinthians 15 v 54, quoting Isaiah 25 v 8)

In this illumination, the pearl in the centre speaks of the purity and holiness of this light that is shining. The sapphires represent heaven, and remind us that this is a divine light that has come from heaven to earth. This silver light edges the dark shapes to remind us that God's light and holiness reach out into the darkness to call sinners to repentance and receive the light of life.

So, 'the light shines in the darkness . . .' but what is *our* response? Do we *turn towards* the light and follow Jesus, or do we *turn away*?

A PAUSE FOR THOUGHT . . .

Gilded Labyrinth

Gold leaf on paper

GILDED LABYRINTH

Labyrinths have long been used as an aid to prayer and meditation, and in the last few decades there has been a revival of interest.

A Labyrinth is not the same as a Maze. Unlike a Maze, a Labyrinth has no T-junctions or cross-roads where choices have to be made, and there are no dead ends. A Labyrinth has only one path, and by following it, one *will* reach the centre. There are twists and turns, and at times we appear to move away from our aimed for destination at the centre, but we must trust the path. There is one way to follow. Jesus said, 'I am the way and the truth and the life. No-one comes to the Father except through me.' (John 14 v 6)

The fact that there is no choice of path is a reminder that God has a purpose for each of His children, but we are not to be passive and just let things happen. As we walk along the path of life, we need to pray, seeking guidance in decision-making, and trusting God to lead us.

'Whether you turn to the right or to the left, your ears will hear a voice behind you, saying, "This is the way; walk in it."' (Isaiah 30 v 21)

'" . . . For I know the plans I have for you," declares the Lord, "plans to prosper you and not to harm you, plans to give you hope and a future."' (Jeremiah 29 v 11)

The Labyrinth is to be regarded as a 'tool': it does not have magical power in itself to be a solver of problems…but if we approach it in the right way it can be 'a Place of Grace' where the Holy Spirit can continue His work of transformation in our lives. The Labyrinth provides an opportunity for time with God, and for Him to 'illuminate' our thoughts; it is pictured here as a golden path.

While Labyrinths are meant to be physically walked, if we do not have access to one, we can use a printed one as a 'finger labyrinth', following the path with our finger.

Here are two ways that we can use a Labyrinth as a Place of Grace:

A Place to Pray
We can walk the Labyrinth to take time with God in prayer. We may be seeking guidance on a particular question, asking God to 'illuminate' the path we should take.
'I will instruct you and teach you in the way you should go; I will counsel you and watch over you.' (Psalm 32 v 8).
'Your word is a lamp to my feet and a light for my path.' (Psalm 119 v 105)

We can use it as a time to meditate on a particular verse or passage of scripture. Alternatively, we can just walk and listen; we don't need to have a predetermined agenda for our time walking the Labyrinth.

As we begin the journey inwards, we will want to focus our minds on God, and imagine leaving anything that might distract us at the entrance. As we walk, we begin to meditate on the verse we have chosen, or lay the concern or decision we need to make, before God. Alternatively, we can simply ask the Holy Spirit to lead our thoughts as we walk. As we walk, and upon reaching the centre, we listen. When we are ready, we begin the outward walk, following the path, and responding to any insights, challenges or encouragements we have received, which we can take out into our lives.

Seeing the Labyrinth as a picture of the pilgrimage of our life-long walk with God
We can think of the Labyrinth as representing our walk with God throughout our lives, with the centre being heaven. As we walk we can reflect on our life-long journey with Him, and maybe take stock of where we are at the present time.
Some people spend their whole lives skirting around the edge of the Labyrinth, but never actually take the step of faith onto it. The beginning is the only place where there is a 'junction', where a decision has to be made: the choice is whether to enter the Labyrinth and walk with God, or not. When we are standing at the beginning, outside the pathway, before taking the step of faith onto the labyrinth, we can think of Jeremiah's words:
'This is what the Lord says: "Stand at the cross roads and look; ask for the ancient paths, ask where the good way is, and walk in it, and you will find rest for your souls . . ."' (Jeremiah 6 v 16)
The labyrinth represents the ancient path, the good way, the way of grace. Again, remember Jesus' words, 'I am the way, and the truth and the life'. (John 14 v 6)

We can learn about walking the Labyrinth as a pilgrimage, reflecting on our life and walk of faith, from the Psalmist:
'Blessed are those whose strength is in you,
who have set their hearts on pilgrimage.
As they pass through the Valley of Baca,
they make it a place of springs;
the autumn rains also cover it with pools.
They go from strength to strength,
till each appears before God in Zion.'
(Psalm 84 v 5 - 7)

To make Pilgrimage is to recognise that we are on a journey, and to be open to be changed by the experience and the different things we face on that journey.
There are blessings to be received and enjoyed by those making pilgrimage: blessed are those who trust in God to sustain them, and whose desire is to 'journey' to know Him better through whatever they must face on the path of life.

The Valley of Baca is unknown, but may represent a dry, arid place. ('Baca' can mean 'weeping'). However, for those walking with God, even in the dry times and the times of suffering, there can be blessings. The 'springs' in the psalm can be seen to represent these blessings from God, and we know from Romans 5 v 3 - 5 that suffering can produce all kinds of positive things in us if we are open to the working of the Holy Spirit. These can be blessings that we receive, but we can also be a blessing to others who are in the 'Valley of Baca'. In fact, Paul encouraged the Corinthians to do this:
"Praise be to the God and Father of our Lord Jesus Christ, the Father of compassion and the God of all comfort, who comforts us in all our troubles, so that we can comfort those in any trouble with the comfort we ourselves have received from God." (2 Corinthians 1 v 3 - 4)

When we are in the place of suffering, the challenge is this: can we join with Job and say to the Lord, 'Blessed be your Name!'? (Job 1 v 21b). It is hard, and we may struggle to do this, but God is full of compassion, and even the place of suffering can be a Place of Grace. Indeed, it can be a time when we are more aware than ever of the care and presence of our Lord.

Also, notice from these verses, that the pilgrims 'pass through' the Valley of Baca: they don't stay there, because their sights are set on reaching their final destination. However, in order to reach it, they must pass through this dry valley.

When we encounter difficulties, disappointments or suffering, are we prone to sit with our head in our hands and say, 'That's it then! The path stops here.'? Or do we remember to keep our focus on our long term destination? Yes, it may be a struggle, but those who keep on going on their pilgrimage with the Lord, eyes fixed on their destination, find they are able to do so. In fact, they 'go from strength to strength' (v 7) because of the help of the Lord God, who 'is a sun and shield' (v 11).

Sometimes life will be difficult, but the only way forward is to trust God and trust His path:
'Trust in the Lord with all your heart and lean not on your own understanding; in all your ways acknowledge him, and he will make your paths straight.' (Proverbs 3 v 5 - 6)

Unlike the Psalmist in Psalm 84, when we set our hearts on pilgrimage and on coming to know God better through prayer, we do not have to go to a physical place where God dwells in order to be with God. Through Jesus we can be in the presence of God wherever we are, in that 'Place of Grace'.

A PAUSE FOR THOUGHT . . .

A Well-Watered Garden

Watercolour on paper

A WELL-WATERED GARDEN

This painting shows a flourishing garden in the midst of a desert, and can be seen as a picture of a Christian surrounded by the secular world.

In chapter 58 of Isaiah, the Lord spoke against the hypocrisy of His people and how this attitude hindered their prayers and their whole relationship with Him. He called them to true repentance and humble service, and promised:

'The LORD will guide you always; he will satisfy your needs in a sun-scorched land and will strengthen your frame.
You will be like a well-watered garden, like a spring whose waters never fail.'
(Isaiah 58 v 11)

The Lord gave a stark warning, and a wonderful promise through Jeremiah: 'This is what the LORD says: "Cursed is the one who trusts in man . . . whose heart turns away from the LORD. He will be like a bush in the wastelands; . . . he will dwell in the parched places of the desert . . . But blessed is the man who trusts in the LORD, whose confidence is in him. He will be like a tree planted by the water that sends out its roots by the stream. It does not fear when heat comes; its leaves are always green. It has no worries in a year of drought and never fails to bear fruit."' (Jeremiah 17 v 5 - 8)

Elsewhere in Jeremiah we read about how shocking it is that God's people have deserted Him and turned to other sources of satisfaction, only to find that they are deeply disappointed:
'"Be appalled at this, O heavens . . . ," declares the LORD, "My people have committed two sins: They have forsaken me, the spring of living water, and have dug their own cisterns, broken cisterns that cannot hold water."'
(Jeremiah 2 v 12 - 13)

Why is the world as it is? Why is it depicted as a desert? Because its people have forsaken God, and have tried to meet their own needs. However, these things do not satisfy, and so they are left without hope, like lost sheep, without a shepherd, blind, in darkness, slaves to passions and pleasures. Life lived in that way is like a dry, parched desert.

Life-giving water

Returning to the picture of the flourishing garden: how can the plants survive in the arid conditions that surround it? It has its own special water supply: it is watered by a spring in the centre of the little garden, resulting in healthy, fruitful plants.

Similarly, how can Christians flourish in a world which has turned its back on God and lives by secular values? Jesus graciously gives us a source of life-giving refreshment. There are two aspects to this:

In his conversation with a Samaritan woman, Jesus said He could give her 'living water' (John 4 v10). He continued: ' . . . whoever drinks the water I give . . . will never thirst. Indeed, the water I give him will become in him a spring of water welling up to eternal life.' (John 4 v 14)

This 'living water' is the abundant, full, eternal life that only the Good Shepherd can give (John 10 v 10).

Later, Jesus spoke of this 'living water' again, with another wonderful truth: ' . . . Jesus stood and said in a loud voice, "If anyone is thirsty, let him come to me and drink. Whoever believes in me, as the Scripture has said, streams of living water will flow from within him." By this he meant the Spirit whom those who believed in him were later to receive.' (John 7 v 37 - 39)

The remarkable truth is that God lives in His people by His Holy Spirit, who, in turn, enables us to live as His people. Jesus promised that the Father would give the Holy Spirit, describing Him as a 'Counsellor to be with you forever - the Spirit of truth . . . when he . . . comes, he will guide you into all truth.' (John 14 v 16 - 17 and 16 v 13)

The Holy Spirit establishes us in our faith, and His indwelling sets us apart as God's possession: 'Now it is God who makes both us and you stand firm in Christ. He anointed us, set his seal of ownership on us, and put his Spirit in our hearts as a deposit, guaranteeing what is to come.' (2 Corinthians 1 v 21 - 22)

He it is who sanctifies us, making us holy, through the cleansing blood of Christ (see 1 Peter 1 v 2). He helps us to pray, and even intercedes for us (Romans 8 v 26 - 27). He equips us to serve (Ephesians 6 v 10 - 18), strengthens and encourages the church (Acts 9 v 31), and wonderfully grows His 'fruit' in our lives (Galatians 5 v 22 - 23, and see the meditation 'The Tree of Psalm 1', pages 56 -57). He gives us a rhythm to live by: 'Since we live by the Spirit, let us keep in step with the Spirit.' (Galatians 5 v 25)

Encircling Presence

A fence surrounds the garden, as a reminder of the encircling of God's presence around us in the Place of Grace. As we read in Scripture:
'You are my hiding-place; you will protect me from trouble and surround me with songs of deliverance . . . many are the woes of the wicked, but the LORD's unfailing love surrounds the man who trusts in him.'
(Psalm 32 v 7 & 10)

'The angel of the LORD encamps around those who fear him, and he delivers them.' (Psalm 34 v 7)

'As the mountains surround Jerusalem, so the LORD surrounds his people both now and for evermore.' (Psalm 125 v 2)

In 1 Kings 6 we read about what happened when Elisha was surrounded by an army intent on capturing him. When his servant saw the forces surrounding the city he was dismayed, but Elisha said, '"Don't be afraid . . . Those who are with us are more than those who are with them." And Elisha prayed, "O LORD, open his eyes so that he may see." Then the LORD opened the servant's eyes, and he looked and saw the hills full of horses and chariots of fire all around Elisha.' (2 Kings 6 v 16 - 17)
John similarly encouraged his readers to remember the unseen reality of God's presence with his people: ' . . . the one who is in you is greater than the one who is in the world.' (1 John 4 v 4)

The Celtic tradition has a type of prayer called a 'Caim' prayer, which asks for the encircling protection of God around a person or place. It is prayed while drawing an imaginary circle around the person or place being committed to God's care, and asks that opposing qualities would be kept without and within the circle.

Encircle me, Lord:
Keep evil without, keep goodness within;
Keep hatred without, keep love within;
Keep fear without, keep trust within;
Keep turmoil without, keep calm within;
Keep despair without, keep hope within;
Keep storms without, keep peace within;
Keep hatred without, keep love within;
Keep bitterness without, keep grace within.
Amen.

A Place of Grace for Others

Continuing with the thought that A Place of Grace is a picture of the blessed state of the Christian soul, this painting also considers how we can be A Place of Grace and a source of blessing to others, as well. A Christian can be a well-watered garden, but we live in the arid desert of spiritual complacency in the world.

Notice how the stream of God's Spirit and grace flows out from the garden into the desert and the result is new growth! Through humble service and Christian love in action, we can be a blessing to others, and this can point people to our Lord Jesus Christ . . . and new gardens begin to grow . . .

The garden has a boundary, but it is not a high wall that completely cuts it off from its surroundings; it is in the desert, but not of the desert. The boundary is a low picket fence, which allows those who are outside to see something of the beauty of the garden inside. This is a reminder of a line from the hymn, 'Dear Lord and Father of mankind':
'Let our ordered lives confess the beauty of thy peace.'
While we probably feel that our lives are far from this ideal, hopefully there will be something very attractive and different about our lives, and how we deal with what we encounter through life, that will be noticed by others and recognised as the Lord's influence . . .

For further contemplation on these themes, consider these verses:
'"Surely God is my salvation; I will trust and not be afraid.
The LORD, the LORD, is my strength and my song;
he has become my salvation."
With joy you will draw water from the wells of salvation.' (Isaiah 12 v 2 - 3)

'Praise be to the God and Father of our Lord Jesus Christ, the Father of compassion, and the God of all comfort, who comforts us in all our troubles, so that we can comfort those in any trouble with the comfort we ourselves have received from God.' (2 Corinthians 1 v 3 - 4)

LESSONS FROM NATURE

In medieval thought, Nature was viewed as a 'book' through which God taught humanity, revealing truths about Himself, so it was natural for medieval craftsmen to take inspiration from what they saw around them, and how it reflected something of God's truth. It is good to recognise God's hand in Creation, and to thank Him for its beauty. God has many lessons to teach us from nature:

'For since the Creation of the world God's invisible qualities - his eternal power and divine nature - have been clearly seen, being understood from what has been made, so that men are without excuse.' (Romans 1 v 20).

When we take time to notice what is all around us - from the vastness of the universe to the details of a tiny flower - when we marvel and remember our Creator, when we look and listen for what He is saying, then we can find ourselves in a Place of Grace.

I often look to nature for inspiration for my work: the next piece is a meditation on God's great act of Creation. This is followed by two illuminations that are based on details in the natural world.

Flower of Creation

Gold leaf, shell gold and watercolour on paper

with pearls and sapphires

FLOWER OF CREATION

Geometry is a universal language, and the geometric structure of this piece is found in the decorative art of many different cultures worldwide. The pattern is the natural division of a circle by its own radius, which divides the circumference exactly into six. If these points are joined together they form a hexagon. It is sometimes referred to as 'The Flower of Creation' because it is formed of six circles around a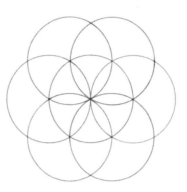
seventh, a reminder of the six days of Creation and the seventh of rest.

In this piece each day of Creation is depicted in the six outer circles, drawing on the visual language found in medieval decorative art:

- In Genesis 1 v 2 we read that 'the Spirit of God was hovering over the waters' and is represented in gold in the dark blue triangle at the top. To make clear that the great act of Creation had Divine initiative, the hand of Almighty God is shown reaching down from heaven, (as found in medieval manuscripts to indicate God's direct action), and pointing to the beginning, on the first day: 'Let there be light'.
- The creation of the sky on the second day is depicted by a highly stylised form of clouds found in medieval art.
- The third day saw the formation of the land and the sea, followed by vegetation.
- The sun, moon and stars first lit up the heavens on the fourth day.
- On the fifth day the waters began to teem with life, and birds filled the air. The birds depicted here are drawn from medieval tile designs.
- The living creatures who appeared on the sixth day are represented by a lion in typical heraldic pose, and the faces of the man and woman are in a style that is characteristic of medieval stained glass.
- The central circle in gold represents the seventh day of rest, blessed by God and made holy, and pointing to God's offer and promise of salvation: to enter a rest that is spiritual and eternal, where everything will be 'made new' (Revelation 21 v 1 and 5) - surely the ultimate Place of Grace, at peace with God. (See pages 64 - 75 , The Heavenly Jerusalem)

The pearl at the centre represents the purity and holiness of God and those at the outer intersections of the circles remind us of the perfection of his Creation 'in the beginning.' The sapphires at the inner intersections of the circles represent heaven (see the central circle and seventh day, above).

The account of Creation in Genesis is not meant to be a scientific paper describing how the world came into being. It is to tell us that it did not come about by chance, but was planned by a loving Creator, and made with care and purpose.

The wonders of Creation should point us to the Creator and tell us of God. We can look around us and see the character of God reflected in what He has made. Majestic grandeur, delicate perfection, care over tiny details, beauty and splendour all reflect His awesome power, wisdom and love. Creation bears witness to the Creator for all people:
'The heavens declare the glory of God; the skies proclaim the work of his hands. Day after day they pour forth speech; night after night they display knowledge. There is no speech or language where their voice is not heard.' (Psalm 19 v 1 - 3)

'For since the Creation of the world God's invisible qualities - his eternal power and divine nature - have been clearly seen, being understood from what has been made, so that men are without excuse.' (Romans 1 v 20).

Since God is Creator of all, we are to take careful note of nature, for it speaks of God. The psalmist knew this, and Psalm 19 tells how Creation proclaims God's glory in a way that is understandable in all languages, and 'to the ends of the world'. Romans 1 v 20 also cautions us against ignoring what is plain to see in Creation about the Divine nature.

Pondering the wonder of Creation should lead us to worship God. Let us not take nature for granted, but open our eyes to the beauty of the world around us, recognising God's fingerprints in what He has made, and regularly give thanks to our Creator God.

We have a responsibility to care for the world which God entrusted to us as stewards, and to seek to live in His world in His way.

'God saw all that he had made, and it was very good.' (Genesis 1 v 31). God's Creation was totally and wonderfully perfect; it was without fault. Sadly, it has not remained in that state of perfection: we have abused it and spoilt it. Genesis 3 relates what is referred to as The Fall, when mankind opted to live independently of God, with catastrophic results: separation from God and His blessings. All around us Creation is not the perfection it was in the beginning: the bad parts of life and how they affect Creation are consequences of the Fall.

The prophet Hosea wrote:
'There is no faithfulness, no love, no acknowledgement of God in the land. There is only cursing, lying and murder, stealing and adultery; they break all bounds, and bloodshed follows bloodshed. Because of this the land mourns, and all who live in it waste away; the beasts of the field and the birds of the air and the fish of the sea are dying.' (Hosea 4 v 1 - 3).

This was written to challenge God's people in Hosea's day, but it also rings true for today. The terrible results of broken human relationships in turn affect Creation, but it all begins with the failure to acknowledge God and to live in His world in His way. However, there is hope - there is a way back: God's words of judgement to the serpent for enticing humanity include the promise of One who will 'crush his head' (Genesis 3 v 15). This defeat of Satan was fulfilled by our Lord Jesus Christ in His death and resurrection. The full effects of this defeat will only be experienced in Eternity, but until then we can know the blessing of a restored relationship with God: 'Therefore, since we have been justified through faith, we have peace with God through our Lord Jesus Christ . . . ' (Romans 5 v 2)

A Prayer

O God, this world is so full of treasures and pleasures; please forgive us when we allow them to distract us and take priority in our lives.
May we rightly enjoy and use the gifts and blessings you give to us, and may we do so with grateful hearts and a generous spirit.
Let us see your beautiful Creation as a constant reminder of your greatness as the Creator, and your care as the Sustainer of the world, and remember that one day you will make all things new. Please help us to care for Creation responsibly.
May our wonder at the distance of the stars, our awe at the majestic grandeur of the mountains and our pleasure at the beauty of a tiny flower lead us to worship you from the depths of our heart and soul, and give ourselves to serve you faithfully and live in your ways.
Amen.

Apple Blossom Illumination

Gold leaf, shell gold and watercolour on vellum

with rubies and pearl.

APPLE BLOSSOM ILLUMINATION

This piece was inspired by a medieval tile in Malvern Priory, and apple trees in springtime. The beautiful five-fold pattern is reminiscent of a rose window, although it is actually from a fifteenth century floor tile. It has the same geometry as apple blossom, whose petals are almost circular. The centre of the pattern reflects the gaps between the petals, and also a cross-section through the core of an apple.

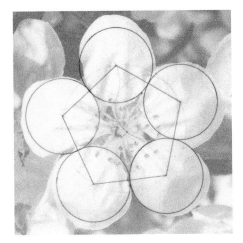
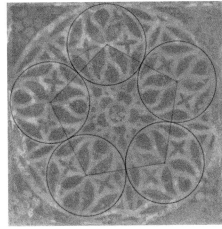

In spring the trees are clothed in the beautiful fresh green of their foliage before the blossom appears. At first the buds are deep pink in colour, and these are represented in the pattern with pink dots. Wonderfully, as the buds open, the petals are transformed into almost pure white, so some squares have a motif of five white dots, reflecting this. This could bring to mind the Lord's gracious words in Isaiah 1 v 18 which are a reminder of forgiveness available through faith in Christ: '"Come now, let us reason together," says the LORD. "Though your sins are like scarlet, they shall be as white as snow . . ."'

The ten gold quatrefoils have tiny rubies in their centres, representing the hope of rosy-red apples to be enjoyed later in the year. The Christian hope (which is sure and certain) is of eternal life to be enjoyed in God's presence: the ultimate Place of Grace:

'Praise be to the God and Father of our Lord Jesus Christ! In his great mercy he has given us new birth into a living hope through the resurrection of Jesus Christ from the dead, and into an inheritance that can never perish, spoil or fade - kept in heaven for you, who through faith are shielded by God's power until the coming of the salvation that is ready to be revealed in the last time.' (1 Peter 1 v 3 - 5)

Passiflora Rose Window

Watercolour and shell palladium on paper

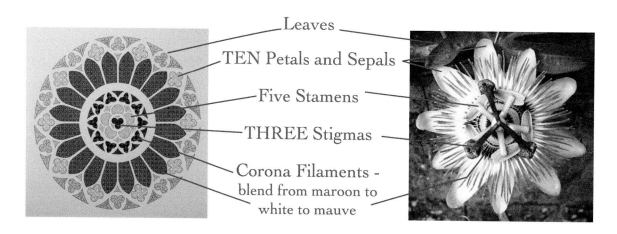

Leaves

TEN Petals and Sepals

Five Stamens

THREE Stigmas

Corona Filaments -
blend from maroon to
white to mauve

PASSIFLORA ROSE WINDOW

The wonderfully exotic and sculptural Passion Flower (passiflora caerulea) has a rich tradition of Christian meaning dating back to the sixteenth century, when Spanish missionaries found it in its native South America. Studying the flower while contemplating the symbolism may lead to a meditation on the Cross of Christ and His sacrifice for us. I have sought to represent this symbolism in a rose window of my own design.

TEN - At first glance it looks like a ten petalled flower, but it is in fact formed of five petals and five sepals, which are white tinged with green. Traditionally they represent the ten faithful disciples - not including Judas, who betrayed Jesus, or Peter who denied Him. However, it is helpful to remember the grace with which Peter was restored after the resurrection. That same grace is extended to each one of us who will repent and trust in Christ.

FIVE - the five stamens represent the five wounds of Christ. The Catholics of South America call the Passion Flower 'The Flower of the Five Wounds'. Each stamen is shaped rather like a hammer, recalling the hammer used to drive in the nails.
'But he was pierced for our transgressions, he was crushed for our iniquities; the punishment that brought us peace was upon him, and by his wounds we are healed.' (Isaiah 53 v 5)

THREE - Above the stamens are three stigmas which represent the three nails used to crucify our Lord Jesus Christ. The three bracts around the buds (not illustrated) represent the Trinity.

The CORONA FILAMENTS symbolise the crown of thorns with a blood red inner fringe. Think about the cruel mockery Jesus suffered, and that He is not just *a* king, He is the King of kings . . .

The TENDRILS represent the whips used to flog Jesus before crucifixion, or the cords of His bondage.

The LEAVES are shaped like the head of a spear, reminding us that the centurion pierced the body of Christ to confirm that He had died.

COLOURS - the blue of the filaments symbolise heaven, and the white filaments and petals remind us of the purity of Christ and His sacrifice.

The flower blooms for one day - the time Christ suffered on the cross. Then the petals close, taken to represent Christ in the tomb. The dead flower is then transformed into the fruit, a reminder of Christ's resurrection. The fruit can also be taken to represent the world that Christ came to save.

THREE TREES

Trees are a wonderful and majestic part of God's Creation and they are beautiful in every season:

- They have a fresh mantle of green in the Spring, sometimes with blossom as well. What a joy it is to see those first few leaves bursting forth after the coldness and starkness of Winter.
- In Summer there is mature and healthy foliage, and for some trees this season culminates with lovely fruit.
- Then follow the stunning colours of Autumn: such beauty, even in decay.
- In Winter we can enjoy seeing the silhouette of the branches, especially against a cold, pale, wintry sky, tinged with pink. There is a lesson for us in this apparently lifeless silhouette, for the buds of next year's leaves are already there to be seen, even in the depths of Winter. They may have to endure harsh weather and sharp frosts, but they stand witness to the sure hope that Spring will follow Winter: there is the promise of new life . . . mornings of joy will follow evenings of tearfulness.

The next three Illuminated Meditations are based around three trees that are found in the Bible:

- In Psalm 1 the person who delights in God's words and ways is pictured as a healthy tree.
- The Cross of Christ: a Tree of Life.
- The Tree of Life in the Book of Revelation.

The Tree of Psalm 1

Gold leaf and watercolour on vellum

THE TREE OF PSALM 1

The tree in Psalm 1 is a picture of a spiritually healthy Christian:
'Blessed is the man who does not walk in the counsel of the wicked or stand in the way of sinners or sit in the seat of mockers.
But his delight is in the law of the LORD, and on his law he meditates day and night.
He is like a tree planted by streams of water, which yields its fruit in season and whose leaf does not wither.
Whatever he does prospers.' (Psalm 1 v 1 - 3)

This is a marvellous picture of a Christian person growing and living in a Place of Grace - in the life of faith and daily dependence on God, trusting in His promises, and submitting to His ways in humility. If we are living in this way, in the Place of Grace, we will not be walking/standing/sitting with those described in verse 1: we will not be following their ways. Instead of seeking counsel and advice from 'the wicked' (v1), we look to God's words and ways for guidance; we will find blessing nowhere else.

In the spandrels of the arch are the sun and the moon, placing this in time - in this world - for we read in Revelation that there will be no more night and no need for the light of the sun, for the Lord God will be the light (see Revelation 22 v 5). The sun and moon shed light, reminding us that we need God's light to give us understanding as we read and meditate on His word.

The Psalmists knew the value of meditating on God's words, and Psalm 119 is full of reasons why we should do so: 'I have hidden your word in my heart that I might not sin against you . . . Your word is a lamp to my feet and a light for my path.' (Psalm 119 v 11 and 105)

We are to meditate on God's words, allowing them to become part of our being, and putting them into practice.

The tree in the illumination is healthy and flourishing because it is planted by streams of water. It is clean, healthy water - there are fish living in it! In the same way, Christians need to root their lives in the Word of God - both His Living Word, our Lord Jesus Christ, and His written word in the Bible: as Paul reminds us in Colossians 2 v 6 - 7:
'So then, just as you received Christ Jesus as Lord, continue to live in him, rooted and built up in him, strengthened in the faith as you were taught, and overflowing with thankfulness.'

Jesus himself is the source of living water:
' " . . . whoever drinks the water I give him will never thirst. Indeed, the water I give him will become in him a spring of water welling up to eternal life . . . If anyone is thirsty, let him come to me and drink. Whoever believes in me, as the Scripture has said, streams of living water will flow from within him." By this he meant the Spirit, whom those who believed in him were later to receive.' (John 4 v 14 and 7 v 37 - 39)

God's words sustain us, and His promises encourage us, helping us through times when life is difficult. A tree with a poor root system is likely to be blown over when storms and high winds hit. Jesus warned of the danger for anyone who has no root in Him in the Parable of the Sower:
'Those on the rock are the ones who receive the word with joy when they hear it, but they have no root. They believe for a while, but in the time of testing they fall away.' (Luke 8 v 13)

The Christian who is rooted in Christ has all the resources and nourishment they need to grow, and do not need anything extra from outside of Christ.
Just as a plant puts roots down so that it can grow up, flourish and produce fruit, so a Christian with firm spiritual roots will grow up and reach out to others in love and service. The way of life that is rooted in Christ yields fruit which is a blessing to those around us. The nine fruits depicted on the tree are a reminder of the nine-fold fruit of the Spirit: ' . . . the fruit of the Spirit is love, joy, peace, patience, kindness, goodness, faithfulness, gentleness and self-control. Against such things there is no law.' (Galatians 5 v 22 - 23)

These are such beautiful qualities! It is worth taking a little time to think about each one, and asking for the Holy Spirit to bring them forth in our lives:
Love - Surely the 'supreme' fruit, from which all the others grow. Jesus said that the two most important commandments were to love God and to love our neighbour (see Mark 12 v 28 - 34), and Paul called love 'the greatest' (see 1 Corinthians 13).
Joy - deep down, joy can always be there for a Christian, even in difficult times, because we know and rely on God's promises, and we know we are loved by Him. We might not necessarily feel joyful all the time, but it is there, deep in our hearts. This kind of joy, Christian joy, is not dependent on circumstances, (in the way that happiness is); instead it springs from the knowledge that we are secure in God's love.
Peace - Like joy, peace is one of those 'deep down' qualities, somehow still there even in the toughest times. On a cloudy day we can still see the effect of the sunshine, even though its brightness is dimmed by clouds. Likewise, in unsettling times, God's peace can help us to keep calm, if we will allow it.

Patience - taking time with someone to put them at ease, making allowances for others, bearing with one another in love. Impatience betrays our selfishness and unwillingness to be put out for the sake of others.

Kindness - a lovely and possibly rather overlooked quality in the eyes of the world. It is a modest quality that doesn't require costly, extravagant gestures - often quite the opposite. It can be expressed in very small, simple ways, and yet have a significant effect for those on the receiving end. A smile and a 'Thank you' to the cashier who serves you, could help them through a long, tiring day. Or think of the difference a kind smile from a stranger can make for someone who is feeling low. Unkindness is, sadly, far too prevalent in society today, especially on social media.

Goodness - in the same way that light shows up best in the dark, so goodness is often seen most clearly against the backdrop of a bad situation.

Faithfulness - we are so weak and prone to fail, but let us look to God, the supreme example of faithfulness, to inspire us.

Gentleness - strength under control. As with the other fruit, growing in gentleness takes time.

Self-control - a quality that brings forth other fruits such as patience and kindness, and can keep us from falling into sin, such as unkind words spoken in haste.

Note that in bringing forth the fruit, the tree does not suffer - the tree's leaves do not wither, for its roots are in 'streams of water'. (However, we can become 'burnt out' if we try to do things in our own strength.)

In Jeremiah 17 v 5 - 8 there is a similar description of a flourishing tree as a picture of one who trusts in the Lord and His limitless resources, even in difficult circumstances. In contrast, those who turn away from God are like a parched bush in the desert. (This is discussed further in 'A Well-Watered Garden' page 39)

Living Cross - Tree of Life

Gold leaf, shell gold and watercolour on paper

with pearls and ruby

LIVING CROSS - TREE OF LIFE

This piece was inspired by an illumination in a Psalter dating from the thirteenth century. The symbolism is very straightforward: the stark wooden cross of Good Friday has become a Tree of Life by Easter Sunday, sprouting abundant foliage. This has come about through the death and resurrection of Jesus Christ.

'Praise be to the God and Father of our Lord Jesus Christ! In his great mercy he has given us new birth into a living hope through the resurrection of Jesus Christ from the dead, and into an inheritance that can never perish, spoil or fade - kept in heaven for you, who through faith are shielded by God's power until the coming of the salvation that is ready to be revealed in the last time.' (1 Peter 1 v 3 - 5)

The stylised rock at the base of the cross shows that this is an earthly event. However, the gold background indicates something in the heavenly realm. This event is, as it were, on the threshold between earth and heaven, and it is of eternal significance.

The pearls used in the piece represent purity - the purity of Christ and His sacrifice; the ruby represents His blood, shed for us for the forgiveness of our sins. Through His death and resurrection, our Lord Jesus Christ has opened the way to heaven and eternal life for all who will believe and trust in Him: 'Death has been swallowed up in victory.' (1 Corinthians 15 v 54) He is 'the way and the truth and the life' (John 14 v 6): He is the way in to the Place of Grace.

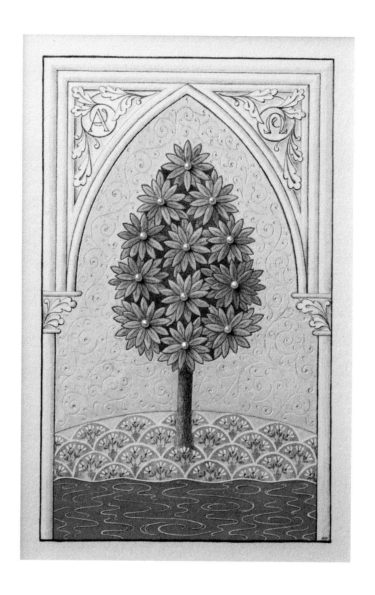

The Tree of Life in the Book of Revelation

Gold leaf, shell gold and watercolour on vellum with pearls

THE TREE OF LIFE IN THE BOOK OF REVELATION

'Then the angel showed me the river of the water of life, as clear as crystal, flowing from the throne of God and of the Lamb down the middle of the great street of the city. On each side of the river stood the tree of life, bearing twelve crops of fruit, yielding its fruit every month. And the leaves of the tree are for the healing of the nations.' (Revelation 22 v 1 - 2)

The symbols of Alpha and Omega in the spandrels of the arch, remind us who is Sovereign: '"I am the Alpha and the Omega," says the Lord God, "who is, and who was, and who is to come, the Almighty."'(Revelation 1 v 8) Alpha and Omega are the first and last letters of the Greek alphabet, signifying the complete span from start to finish. God is sovereign over all, from the beginning of history to the end . . . and beyond; He is the One on the throne: 'He who was seated on the throne said, " . . . I am the Alpha and the Omega, the Beginning and the End . . ."' (Revelation 21 v 5 - 6)

The gold background places this scene in heaven: this is the ultimate Place of Grace - the final destination for us at the end of our journey of faith through life. This is something to contemplate when life is hard or when we feel 'spiritually dry' . . . when we need something to encourage us. If we lift our eyes to heaven and remember Who is on the throne, and what awaits us there, it can help us to gain a fresh perspective on our current situation, and we ' . . . find grace to help us in our time of need.' (Hebrews 4 v 16) Let us remember that 'the view from the throne of grace is different'.

In the first of the letters to the churches at the beginning of Revelation, there is the wonderful promise of 'the right to eat from the tree of life, which is in the paradise of God.' (Revelation 2 v 7) The letter says that this is granted to those who 'overcome': that is, those who remain faithful to Jesus to the end, showing patient endurance in the face of persecution, living out their faith in loving service, remaining true to their Saviour and loving Him above all others. The author of Hebrews encourages his readers to live in this way: ' . . . let us throw off everything that hinders and the sin that so easily entangles, and let us run with perseverance the race marked out for us. Let us fix our eyes on Jesus, the author and perfecter of our faith, who for the joy set before him endured the cross, scorning its shame, and sat down at the right hand of the throne of God. Consider him who endured such opposition from sinful men, so that you will not grow weary and lose heart.' (Hebrews 12 v 1 - 3)

Mention of the Tree of Life takes us back to Genesis, where it stands in the middle of the Garden of Eden. The Fall of humanity caused us to be banished from the garden and the chance of reaching out to eat the fruit of this tree . . and yet this is what we long for: this fruit is the only fruit that will truly satisfy us, along with the life-giving water.

Who may eat of this fruit? In Revelation 22 v 14 we read that it is 'those who wash their robes' who 'have the right to the tree of life'. Revelation 7 v 14 explains this further: ' . . . they have washed their robes and made them white in the blood of the Lamb.' 'White robes' symbolise purity, but we cannot attain purity through our own efforts. Only by trusting in the death and resurrection of Jesus can we be forgiven and cleansed from our sin:
'In [Christ] we have redemption through his blood, the forgiveness of sins, in accordance with the riches of God's grace . . . ' (Ephesians 1 v 7) ' . . . and the blood of Jesus . . . purifies us from all sin.' (1 John 1 v 7)

As white robes symbolise purity, so do the pearls that represent the fruit in the painting: this fruit will be perfect and satisfying. There are twelve fruits shown on the tree because, as we read in Revelation 22 v 2, the tree bears ' . . . twelve crops of fruit, yielding its fruit every month.' Twelve is a number associated with perfection, so twelve crops of fruit indicate perfect provision and satisfaction.

We read here that ' . . . the leaves of the tree are for the healing of the nations.' How wonderful it will be when there is true peace and harmony instead of division and strife!

The water in the painting represents the water of life, another gift and privilege for those in white robes to enjoy.

The tree stands on the banks of the river of the water of life, (see Revelation 22 v 1 - 2). This is ' . . . a river whose streams make glad the city of God, the holy place where the Most High dwells.' (Psalm 46 v 4)

(For further thoughts about the leaves of the tree and the water of life, see 'The Heavenly Jerusalem', pages 73 - 74)

A PAUSE FOR THOUGHT . . .

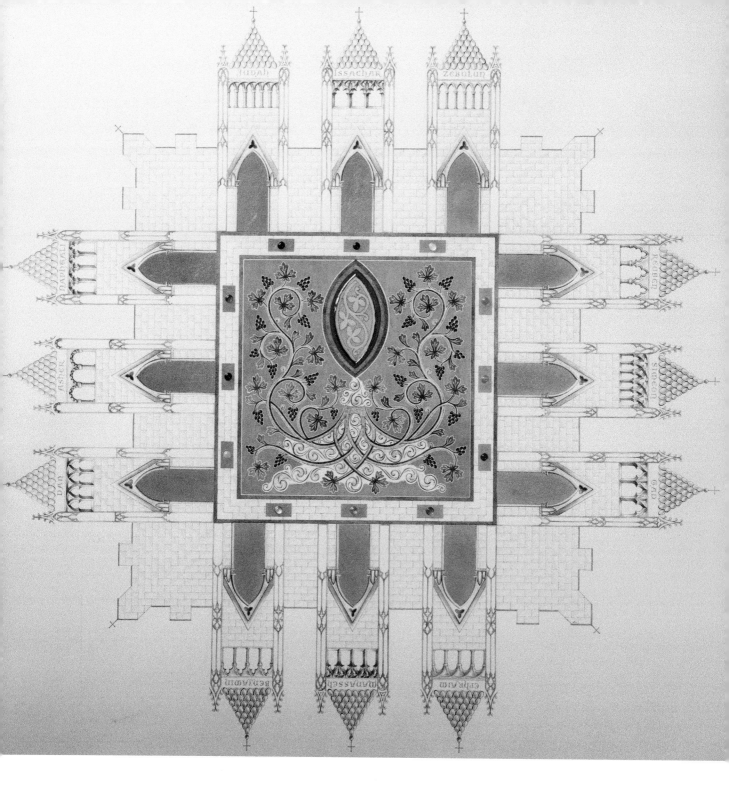

The Heavenly Jerusalem

Gold leaf, shell gold and watercolour on vellum

The identification of some of the stones making up the foundations is
uncertain, or their meaning has changed.
The Cabochons used here are, clockwise from top left:
Jasper, Lapis Lazuli (for *'Sapphire'*), Chalcedony, Emerald,
Sardonyx (*striped Carnelian*), Carnelian, Citrine (for *'Chrysolite'*),
Aquamarine (for *'Beryl'*), Peridot (for *'Topaz'*), Chrysoprase,
Sapphire (for *'Jacinth'*) and Amethyst.

THE HEAVENLY JERUSALEM

And so we arrive at the gates of the Heavenly Jerusalem, the ultimate Place of Grace. Only here will all our longings for peace, security, wholeness, justice, righteousness - and so much more - be satisfied. Truly satisfied. Perfectly satisfied. Eternally satisfied.

We were made for eternity, so the things that belong to 'time', with all the limitations that imposes, cannot satisfy:
' . . . He has also set eternity in the hearts of men; yet they cannot fathom what God has done from beginning to end.' (Ecclesiastes 3 v 11)

The name of the final book of the Bible, Revelation, means 'unveiling', and it is a window onto heaven. The description of the Heavenly City in the final two chapters of the book is astonishing. It is breathtakingly beautiful, and beyond anything we can imagine . . .

Any attempt to depict this vision will fall very short of the awesome description. It was not possible to include all the elements mentioned, but I hope that this piece captures something of the spirit of what we are told, and will at least help us to meditate on certain truths about the final destination of our journey.

The Symbolism of Numbers

Numbers have significance in the Bible as a whole, but they are particularly important in Revelation.

3 - the number of God, who is the Trinity of Father, Son and Holy Spirit. It is beyond the capacity of our minds to understand how God can be One, and yet Three! - but that is part of the mystery of the Divine. (A helpful picture is to think about the compound with the formula H_2O: in whatever form it appears - as a liquid (water), a solid (ice) or a gas (steam or water vapour), it still has the same formula.)

4 - the number of the world. In the beginning there was God, the Trinity. When He created the world, there was another entity in existence, so three plus one is four. This is reflected in four compass points, and four seasons in the year.

7 - 3 (God) + 4 (the world) = 7 (all that exists), so seven is symbolic of completeness and perfection. God rested on the seventh day, because His work of creating was complete. In Revelation we look forward to the Sabbath rest of eternity.

8 - the number of the new creation and eternal life. It speaks of regeneration, a new beginning: one after the completeness of seven. In Revelation we hear that God will 'make everything new'. Jesus rose from the dead on the eighth day (i.e. on the first day of the new week - John 20 v 1), opening the way to eternal life.

10 - the number symbolic of totality, entirety. In the first chapter of Genesis God spoke ten times to bring 'the heavens and the earth' into existence: the entire creation. The entire Law is found in the Ten Commandments.

12 - 3 (God) x 4 (the world) = 12 - God's work in the world, His power and authority. Twelve is a number associated with perfection, and also with leadership, kingdoms and government: there are twelve tribes of Israel, and Jesus appointed twelve apostles. Twelve months make a 'whole' year. Twelve crops of fruit indicate perfect provision and satisfaction. As we will see, twelve is key in the dimensions of the Holy City.

As there is so much to take in, the description is divided into sections.

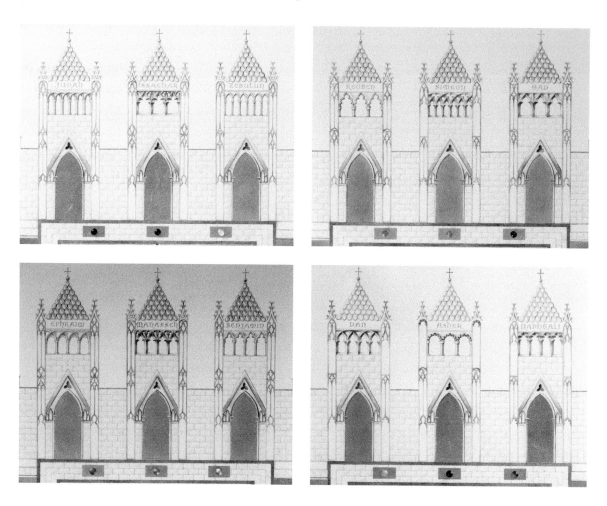

God will dwell with his people

'Then I saw a new heaven and a new earth, for the first heaven and the first earth had passed away, and there was no longer any sea. I saw the Holy City, the new Jerusalem, coming down out of heaven from God, prepared as a bride beautifully dressed for her husband. And I heard a loud voice from the throne saying, "Now the dwelling of God is with men, and he will live with them. They will be his people, and God himself will be with them and be their God. He will wipe every tear from their eyes. There will be no more death or mourning or crying or pain, for the old order of things has passed away." He who was seated on the throne said, "I am making everything new!" Then he said, "Write this down, for these words are trustworthy and true."' (Revelation 21 v 1 - 5)

In this vision of the future, God has made everything 'new'. All that had been spoilt by the effects of the Fall has been restored to the perfection of Eden. There is no longer any sea (v1), for in the Bible, the sea is symbolic of chaos. We learn what else is not present in heaven: death, mourning, crying or pain (v4). This is a reversal of the curses that were the consequences of the Fall, back in Genesis 3.

The question that has been asked throughout the Bible, and throughout history, is this: How can sinful people live in the presence of a holy God? By our own efforts there is no way, but the salvation wrought by Christ in His death and resurrection has made this possible, and in this vision it reaches its completion: God announces that He will dwell with His people. This, too, is a return to Eden, and is possible because all sin and evil has been banished. It is the situation that has been longed for throughout the Bible. It is the fulfilment of all the promises and covenants that God has made. It brings to fruition, in the fullest sense, these words of God, which are repeated time and again through the Scriptures: 'I will be their God, and they will be my people.' (e.g. Leviticus 26 v 12, Jeremiah 31 v 33)

This city is the shape of a cube (described in the next section), and it shines with the glory of God. The Tabernacle in the desert and the Temple in Jerusalem were visual illustrations of the whole creation: the Most Holy Place in both was cuboid, and represented the throne room of heaven; the Holy Place and the courtyard represented the earth. But, the Most Holy Place was separated from the rest of the Tabernacle/Temple by a curtain. When the glory of the LORD filled the Tabernacle (Exodus 40 v 34 - 35), Moses could not enter. When the glory of the LORD filled the Temple (see 2 Chronicles 7 v 1 - 3), the priests could not enter. In the Holy City, however, the dwelling of God is with His people in a new way, and 'They will see his face . . . ' (Revelation 22 v 4) John also observed, 'I did not see a temple in the city, because the Lord God Almighty and the Lamb are its temple.' (Revelation 21 v 22).

The Appearance of the City - its Walls and Gates

John continues describing the vision he received:
'And he carried me away in the Spirit to a mountain great and high, and showed me the Holy City, Jerusalem, coming down out of heaven from God. It shone with the glory of God, and its brilliance was like that of a very precious jewel, like a jasper, clear as crystal. It had a great, high wall with twelve gates, and with twelve angels at the gates. On the gates were written the names of the twelve tribes of Israel. There were three gates on the east, three on the north, three on the south and three on the west. The wall of the city had twelve foundations, and on them were the names of the twelve apostles of the Lamb.

. . . The city was laid out like a square, as long as it was wide . . . 12,000 stadia in length, and as wide and high as it is long. The wall was made of jasper, and the city of pure gold, as pure as glass . . . The twelve gates were twelve pearls, each gate made of a single pearl. The great street of the city was of pure gold, like transparent glass.' (Revelation 21 v 10 - 14, 16, 18, 21)

This city is vast! 12,000 stadia is about 1,400 miles, and it is that dimension in every direction, to form a cube! It is easy to be distracted by the scale of this, and we will concentrate on certain details, but we do need to note the significance of that number. It is 12, (complete, perfect), multiplied by 1,000, which is 10 x 10 x 10, (10 is totality, and this is then cubed, 10^3).

In the illuminated painting, the city is shown in plan form, with the walls 'folded out' flat, and it is partly based on an illumination in The Trinity Apocalypse*, a thirteenth century manuscript. The walls are described as being made of jasper, and yet 'clear as crystal'. Today we think of jasper as being an opaque, red stone, so it is unclear what is meant. The walls are depicted in a fairly plain manner here, to put the focus on the centre of the city.

There are three gates on each side of the city, each bearing the name of one of the tribes of Israel. Their positions are not specified, so the arrangement designated in Numbers 2 for the tribes when they camped around the Tabernacle in the desert, has been used (with 'East' at the top of the painting).

This city is a safe and secure place, not just because of its substantial walls, but because the wicked will be banished: 'Nothing impure will ever enter it, nor will anyone who does what is shameful or deceitful, but only those whose names are written in the Lamb's book of life.' (Revelation 21 v 27) (See also 1 Corinthians 6 v 9 - 10, Galatians 5 v 19 - 21).

* MS R.16.2, fol.25v, Trinity College, Cambridge.

Isaiah wrote about the safety of this Place of Grace:
' . . . we have a strong city; God makes salvation its walls and ramparts . . .
You will keep in perfect peace him whose mind is steadfast, because he trusts
in you. Trust in the LORD for ever, for the LORD, the LORD, is the Rock
eternal.' (Isaiah 26 v 1, 3 - 4)

Jesus also promised a safe Place of Grace for each of His followers to look
forward to:
'Do not let your hearts be troubled. Trust in God; trust also in me. In my
Father's house are many rooms; if it were not so, I would have told you. I am
going there to prepare a place for you . . . I will come back and take you to
be with me . . . I am the way and the truth and the life. No-one comes to the
Father except through me.' (John 14 v 1 - 3, 6)

The gates are made of pearls, although they are not depicted in the gateways
here because they are always open: 'On no day will its gates ever be shut . .'
(Revelation 21 v 25). This is another indication of how safe it will be. The
arches of the gateways in the illumination are filled with gold to give the
impression of looking in and seeing 'the city of pure gold' (v18). The street
of the city is pure gold (Revelation 21 v 21), depicted here in shell gold,
genuine gold paint, as the background to the water and the tree.

The Foundations

'The foundations of the city walls were decorated with every kind of precious stone. The first foundation was jasper, the second sapphire, the third chalcedony, the fourth emerald, the fifth sardonyx, the sixth carnelian, the seventh chrysolite, the eighth beryl, the ninth topaz, the tenth chrysoprase, the eleventh jacinth, and the twelfth amethyst . . . The great street of the city was of pure gold, like transparent glass.' (Revelation 21 v 19 - 21)

This is a beautiful city! The reference to precious stones harks back to Eden, where they were to be found along with gold (Genesis 2 v 11 - 12), and also reminds us of Isaiah 54 v 11 - 14, where God promises the future restoration and glory of Zion. As the names of the tribes of Israel are written on the twelve gates, so the names of the apostles (not shown in the painting) are written on the twelve foundations. This displays the unity of God's people: in the Heavenly City, the people of Israel in the Old Testament and the Church in the New Testament , are one united people.

Thoughts about foundations lead us to reflect on the truth that Jesus Christ is the foundation of our faith (1 Corinthians 3 v 11), as He taught in the parable of the wise and foolish builders (Matthew 7 v 24 - 27).

A cabochon of each stone mentioned is set in the foundations in the painting, with the first, jasper, positioned in the top left beneath the gate with the name of Judah; the other stones follow clockwise around the square. These beautiful stones reflect the glory of God that fills the city. (See Revelation 4 v 3 and 6, and 21 v 11; also Exodus 24 v 9 - 10).

This list of stones is reminiscent of another, back in Exodus 28 v 15 -21, where we read the instructions for the making of the Breastplate to be worn by Aaron and high priests after him: again it is twelve stones set in a square of gold. Although some of the stones are different, it is still a reminder: in the Tabernacle/Temple, the high priest had the role of mediator between heaven and earth. Jesus is now our Great High Priest in heaven, and He is the mediator of the new covenant. (See Hebrews 4 v 14 - 5 v 10, 7 v 11 - 10 v 18, 12 v 22 - 24 to consider this further).

The Throne of God

' . . . The throne of God and of the Lamb will be in the city . . . ' (Revelation 22 v 3)

As the Tabernacle was at the centre of the encampment of the people of Israel in the desert, and the Temple was at the centre of the earthly Jerusalem, so the throne of God is at the centre of the heavenly city.

How does one set about depicting God seated on His throne!? Many medieval depictions of the Holy City do show a figure and/or the Lamb on a throne. In this painting, symbolic language is used to represent God on His throne, in the form of the shape known as a vesica piscis, a pointed oval. It is the shape formed by the overlap of two circles of the same size, with the circumference of each passing through the centre of the other (see right).

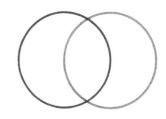

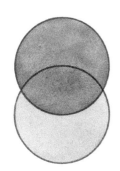

The gold vesica in the illumination represents the glory of God. In medieval thinking the vesica was viewed as representing the portal between heaven and earth; this opening is personified in Christ, the mediator of the New Covenant, through whom is the Way from earth to heaven. Since Christ was fully God and fully human, He is the mediator, the overlap, between heaven and earth. (See left, where the blue circle represents heaven and the green circle, earth. The overlap is a (horizontal) vesica.) For this reason, in medieval art and architecture, the figure of Christ is often placed within a (vertical) vesica, as frequently seen above the entrance to a church or cathedral: it is through Him that we can enter the presence of God.

In this illumination, the vesica shape has been made using the traditional method of applying gold leaf onto a substance called gesso. This gives a slightly raised effect, along with a brilliant shine. This form of gilding was widely used in medieval manuscripts, and this technique is only used for the vesica in this painting, so that it stands out and draws the eye; none of the other gold used in the piece shines as brightly. The whole city is illuminated by the glory of God, which is so great that there is no need for the sun and moon. Jesus, the Light of the World, is also the Light of Heaven: ' . . . the glory of God gives it light, and the Lamb is its lamp.' (Revelation 21 v 23)

There is a pattern impressed into the gold: three tripartite leaves - doubly trinitarian!

The colours that outline the golden vesica represent the three Persons of the Trinity: blue for God the Father, brown for God the Son, and green for God the Holy Spirit. Blue and gold are colours that are commonly associated with God and heaven. Brown is the colour of earth and can represent humility; Jesus humbled himself and dwelt on earth as a man. Green is the colour of life and growth, and is a reminder of the life-giving Spirit of God, who dwells within every believer.

The River of the Water of Life

'Then the angel showed me the river of the water of life, as clear as crystal, flowing from the throne of God and of the Lamb down the middle of the great street of the city . . . Whoever is thirsty, let him come; and whoever wishes, let him take the free gift of the water of life.' (Revelation 22 v 1-2, 17)

Like everything in this city, the river is beautiful: it is pure, its source being the throne of God, and it is 'as clear as crystal'. This is abundant, life-giving water, and it is freely available to all those in the city. Free gifts rarely satisfy, but this one will! This is the ultimate fulfilment of Jesus' promise: '. . . "If anyone is thirsty, let him come to me and drink. Whoever believes in me, as the Scripture has said, streams of living water will flow from within him." By this he meant the Spirit, whom those who believed in him were later to receive.' (John 7 v 37 - 39). The Holy Spirit flows from the throne of the Father and the Son to all in the city.

The Tree of Life
'. . . On each side of the river stood the tree of life, bearing twelve crops of fruit, yielding its fruit every month. And the leaves of the tree are for the healing of the nations.' (Revelation 22 v 2)

Mention of the Tree of Life takes us back to Genesis, where it stands in the middle of the Garden of Eden. The Fall of humanity caused us to be banished from the garden and the chance of reaching out to eat the fruit of this tree - and yet this is what we long for: as Genesis 3 v 22 tells us, anyone who eats the fruit will live for ever.
We are not told how the leaves will provide healing for the nations, but the important thing is that they will heal. It is wonderful to know that one day there will be genuine reconciliation of the divisions that are so apparent among the nations of the world. Only in the perfectly restored Kingdom of God will they no longer be divided, and be able to rest together in peace and harmony.

These verses do not tell us what type of tree it is . . . it will probably be unlike anything we know here on earth. In the painting it is depicted as a vine because that is used as a picture of God's people throughout the Bible: the people of Israel in the Old Testament, and the Church in the New Testament. In the latter, it is Christ who is the vine, 'the true vine', and we, His people, are the branches.

There are twelve leaves and twelve bunches of fruit on each half of the tree, since the tree will produce fruit every month. Twenty four of each, symbolising perfect provision for the whole of God's people from the Old and New Testaments, signified by twelve tribes and twelve apostles. (There are also twelve small leaves on each side, simply to make a balanced, full design.)

Who may enter the city, and eat and drink?
Who may drink this water and eat this fruit? The first of the letters to the churches at the beginning of Revelation, contains the wonderful promise that 'the right to eat from the tree of life, which is in the paradise of God.' (Revelation 2 v 7) will be granted to those who 'overcome': those who remain faithful to Jesus, patiently enduring persecution, living out their faith in loving service, remaining true to their Saviour and loving Him above all others.

However, we cannot do any of this in our own strength. In Revelation 22 v 14 we read that it is 'those who wash their robes' who 'have the right to the tree of life'. Revelation 7 v 14 explains this further: ' . . . they have washed their robes and made them white in the blood of the Lamb.' 'White robes' symbolise purity, but we cannot attain purity through our own efforts. Only by trusting in the death and resurrection of Jesus can we be forgiven and cleansed from our sin: 'In [Christ] we have redemption through his blood, the forgiveness of sins, in accordance with the riches of God's grace . . .' (Ephesians 1 v 7) '. . . and the blood of Jesus . . . purifies us from all sin.' (1 John 1 v 7)

This wonderful salvation cannot be earned, it is pure gift:
'For it is by grace you have been saved, through faith - and this not from yourselves, it is the gift of God - not by works, so that no-one can boast.' (Ephesians 2 v 8 - 9)

This awesome picture of the Heavenly City as our final destination is an encouragement to stand firm in our faith. As Paul wrote to the Colossian church: ' . . . set your hearts on things above, where Christ is seated at the right hand of God. Set your minds on things above, not on earthly things . . When Christ, who is your life, appears, then you also will appear with him in glory.' (Colossians 3 v 1 - 2, 4)

Looking ahead to a time when peace will reign, the Psalmist wrote:
'There will be no breaching of walls, no going into captivity,
no cry of distress in our streets.
Blessed are the people of whom this is true;
blessed are the people whose God is the LORD'
(Psalm 144 v 14 - 15)

To know God, and to dwell in A Place of Grace,
is to be truly blessed!

INDEX OF BIBLE REFERENCES

BIBLIOGRAPHY

NIV Study Bible. Hodder & Stoughton
'The Bible Guide' by Andrew Knowles. Lion Publishing.
'Revelation' by Paul Blackham. 'Book by Book Study Guides' published by Biblical Frameworks.
BST 'The Message of John' by Bruce Milne. IVP

ACKNOWLEDGEMENTS

With grateful thanks to all who have taught me throughout my life - both 'from the pulpit' and 'in the studio'.

Particular thanks to my dear friends Rev'd Beryl Stannard, Juliet Mitchell and Hilary Richardson for their encouragement, proof reading and comments on the text. Needless to say, any errors that remain are mine.

Thanks to Ian Fraser for photographing the Illuminations.

Thanks to all at Orbitpress in Chesham, for help, advice and printing.

Many, many thanks to my family - Mum, Dad, Steve and Chris - for their love, encouragement and support over so many years.

'Who am I? . . . All things come from you, O Lord, and of your own do I give you.' (Paraphrase of 1 Chronicles 29 v 14)

SIZES OF ORIGINAL ILLUMINATIONS

A Place of Grace: 21.3 x 21.3 cm (8 ⅜" x 8 ⅜")
Carpet Page: 17.8 x 11 cm (7" x 4 ⅜")
The Light Shines in the Darkness: 12.8 cm (5") diameter
Gilded Labyrinth: 16 cm (6¼") diameter
A Well-Watered Garden: 19 x 19 cm (7½" x 7½")
Flower of Creation: 14 x 12 cm (5 ½" x 4 ¾")
Apple Blossom Illumination: 12.9 cm (5 ⅛") diameter
Passiflora Rose Window: 14.4 cm (5 ⅝") diameter
The Tree of Psalm 1: 12.8 x 7.9cm (5 x 3 ⅛")
Living Cross - Tree of Life: 10.2 x 7.6 cm (4" x 3")
The Tree of Life in the Book of Revelation: 12.8 x 7.9 cm (5" x 3 ⅛")
The Heavenly Jerusalem: 39 x 39 cm (15¼" x 15¼")

PAUSE FOR REFLECTION . . .

ABOUT HELEN & HER WORK

'I was born and grew up in Chesham, a market town in the beautiful landscape of the Chiltern Hills north west of London. It's where I still live, and I belong to an Anglican Church in the town. After working free-lance as a calligrapher and illuminator for many years, I studied at The Prince's School of Traditional Arts in London, gaining a Master's Degree, with Distinction, in Traditional Arts. I now work as an illuminator and ceramicist. 'A Place of Grace', is my first book, and I'm delighted to be able to share my work in a new way.

My work is characterised by precision and fine detail. Illumination is the use of gold, (or other metals), in either leaf or powdered form; these are applied with the traditional techniques that were used in medieval manuscripts. The addition of tiny semi-precious jewels help to contribute a 'medieval richness' to the work.

My inspiration comes from medieval art, nature and my Christian faith. Through adopting and adapting ideas and principles from medieval sources and natural forms, my aim is to create works that are beautiful, giving pleasure to the viewer, while also expressing Christian truths. I draw on many sources from our wonderful heritage and tradition: in the marinade of creative imagination, visual quotations from medieval tiles, stained glass, fabrics, wood- and stone-carving, as well as manuscripts, are translated into my own work.

At the Prince's School I came to appreciate the principles and practice of geometry, and these have become an important part of my work; they help to bring harmony, beauty and meaning to a composition. The patterns of traditional art reflect nature in a way that is very different from many contemporary artistic practices, and offer a nourishing, complementary alternative.

Medieval craftsmen saw geometry as a reflection of the beauty of Divine order in Creation. They understood that geometry underpins Creation, from the tiniest flower (and smaller) to the movement of the planets. This was reflected in their work as they used the geometry that is the basis of the natural world to express deep symbolic meaning. I see my own work as a continuation of this rich, ancient tradition and way of seeing.'

OLIVE TREE MEDITATIONS is the name under which I publish my books, cards and prints.